DIVINE WHISPERS WITHIN

A DEVOTIONAL PRAYER GUIDE FOR THE SOUL

DR. VERNON D. FRANKLIN

Divine Whispers Within
by Dr. Vernon D. Franklin
Copyright ©2025 Dr. Vernon D. Franklin

ISBN 978-1-63360-322-6

All rights reserved. This book is protected under the copyright laws of the United States of America. This book may not be copied or reprinted for commercial gain or profit.

Scripture quotations marked NIV are taken from THE HOLY BIBLE: New International Version ©1978 by the New York International Bible Society, used by permission of Zondervan Bible Publishers. All rights reserved.

Scripture quotations marked NLT are taken from The Holy Bible, New Living Translation, copyright © 1996, 2004, 2015 by Tyndale House Foundation. Used by permission of Tyndale House Publishers, Inc., Carol Stream, Illinois 60188. All rights reserved.

Scripture quotations marked KJV are taken from THE HOLY BIBLE: King James Version and rest in the public domain.

For Worldwide Distribution   Printed in USA

Urban Press
P.O. Box 5044
Williamsburg, VA 23188
www.urbanpress.us

Table of Contents

Dedication	v
Preface	ix
<u>Prologue</u> The Stillness Within	xiii
Introduction	xx
<u>Chapter One</u> Be Still – God is in His Holy Temple	1
<u>Chapter Two</u> Your Spiritual Umbilical Cord	8
<u>Chapter Three</u> Sacred Place	14
<u>Chapter Four</u> An Awakening	23
<u>Chapter Five</u> Divine Whispers	29
<u>Chapter Six</u> Acts Toward Relationship	37
<u>Chapter Seven</u> When Divine Whispers Reveal UR-Nique Purpose	45
<u>Conclusion</u> The God Who Whispers	50
<u>Epilogue</u> Living in Sacred Rhythm	53
<u>Final Prayer of Blessing</u> Whisper to My Soul	55
Appendix	57

DEDICATION

IN HONOR OF DEACON EDWARD FRANKLIN

AND

DEACONESS SALLIE STEVENS-FRANKLIN

My life has been shaped and influenced by a sacred flow of experiences, teachings, and traditions that began to mold me at an early age. This flow took place within relational circles comprised of family, friends, church leaders, and teachers who all played an important role in my spiritual journey. All this was nurtured by my family's unwavering faith in and commitment to God. This devotional is a testament to and result of their journey that became the foundation for mine.

In my family, faith was more than a theoretical possibility or discussion; it was a way of life. Prayer was expected, church attendance was non-negotiable, and studying the Bible was part of our daily rhythm. At the center of that spiritual foundation were my paternal grandparents, Deacon Edward Franklin and Deaconess Sallie Stevens-Franklin who taught me that true faith wasn't just about going to church but about living in obedience to and trusting in God's divine guidance.

A LEGACY OF FAITH AND RESILIENCE

My grandparents were part of the Great Migration, one of the most significant movements in American history, when millions of Black families left the South in search of a better life and freedom from the harsh grip of Jim Crow laws and customs. Born in neighboring towns in Georgia—my grandfather in Lumpkin and my grandmother in Cuthbert—they carried in their heart a love for the red clay of the land, the pain of injustice, and the hope for something better.

Their journey to Pittsburgh, Pennsylvania wasn't just about economic opportunity, it was also about survival and dignity while creating a more promising future for their children and grandchildren. And even as they faced new struggles in the North, their faith never wavered.

In 1919, with steadfast devotion, they became charter members of Victory Baptist Church, putting down spiritual roots in a city far from their birthplace. What began as a humble Sunday School in their home grew into a thriving congregation. Their resilience and God's faithfulness turned hardship into legacy and their story continues to echo through generations.

They raised seven children while building not just a home, but a spiritual refuge for their community. Through every challenge, they clung to God's promises. No, their faith was not theoretical; they lived it every day.

THE SEED OF DIVINE WHISPERS

My devotion to God stems from seeds planted during those early family devotionals and prayer rituals before meals and bedtimes. These weren't just moments of routine, they were sacred exchanges where I learned the importance of talking to and listening for God. That rhythm of communication in prayer remains with me to this day.

But over time, I discovered that prayer goes beyond words and ritual, formula and duty. Many people assume prayer is just talking to God, listing needs and desires. But my grandparents demonstrated something more profound. I watched them pray with quiet nods, soft groans, and extended silence, as if they were listening to someone. As a child, I thought their silence was attributed to age or fatigue. But now I understand they were engaged in sacred dialogue, listening for God's whispers.

That revelation transformed my understanding of intimacy with God. To know God personally is to enter a two-way relationship—a space where *Divine Whispers* are not only spoken but heard. Thus, this devotional is my tribute to their example:

> *To a faith that stood through storms.*
> *To a legacy that shaped my soul.*
> *And to the sacred rhythm of whispers*
> *Passed down through generations.*
> *Thank you, Gramp and Grandma, for teaching me how to listen.*
> *Thank you for living your faith out loud and in silence.*
> *Your legacy lives on in every whisper I hear.*

PREFACE

In a world full of noise, distractions, and constant demands, *Divine Whispers Within* is an invitation to pause, reflect, and listen to the quiet voice of God speaking within your soul. And make no mistake, God is speaking. This devotional is a journey inward toward the sacred space God created in you for communion, clarity, and peace. We will explore how stillness and spiritual attentiveness awaken your awareness of God's abiding presence and loving guidance. At the center of this journey is my belief that you are God's holy temple, and within your soul, He is always speaking.

Each chapter explores a different layer of what it means to hear and respond to the voice of God in your daily life:

- *Chapter One: Be Still – God is in His Holy Temple*

    Introduces the sacred concept of stillness as a spiritual posture that invites divine presence. It reminds you that your soul is the inner temple where God desires to dwell and speak.

- *Chapter Two: Your Spiritual Umbilical Cord*

  Describes your soul as the sacred lifeline connecting you to God—just as an umbilical cord connects a child to its source of life. It emphasizes that your authentic identity and divine connection began with God's breath, for Genesis 2:7 states,

  > "And the LORD God formed man of the dust of the ground, and breathed into his nostrils the breath of life; and man became a living being."

- *Chapter Three: Sacred Place*

  Uses the metaphor of concentric relational circles to illustrate that only God belongs at the center of your being. It teaches you to guard your sacred space and listen for God's voice.

- *Chapter Four: An Awakening*

  Shares personal stories of unexpected moments when God's presence broke through my ordinary routines. It challenges you to recognize that sacred encounters can happen anywhere and anytime.

- *Chapter Five: Divine Whispers*

  Offers practical insights and personal testimonies on how God speaks through inner promptings. It encourages you to stay attentive and responsive to the gentle nudges of the Holy Spirit.

- *Chapter Six: Acts Toward Relationship*

  Presents four foundational principles: awareness, presence, anticipation, and revelation as essential practices for cultivating a deeper relationship with God and hearing His voice more clearly.

- *Chapter Seven: When God's Whisper Reveals UR-Nique Purpose.*

  This chapter aligns with the theme of discovering your purpose, as presented in my previous book, *UR-Nique Purpose: Three A's to Authenticity*. It addresses a fundamental question you may have asked or be asking: *What is my purpose?* By engaging with the practical principles in this devotional prayer guide, you will start to uncover your unique purpose in your sacred space.

Divine Whispers Within is designed to help you draw nearer to God—not through religious performance, but through relational stillness and sacred attentiveness. There are real-life experiences and guided reflection throughout the devotional, along with devotional prayer guide exercises after each chapter.

My hope is that this devotional prayer guide helps you slow down, quiet the external and internal noise, and tune your heart to the *Divine Whispers* that have always been there guiding, loving, correcting, and calling you deeper. As you read and reflect, may your soul become a sanctuary where God's voice is heard, and your life is transformed.

PROLOGUE

THE STILLNESS WITHIN

Stillness is often misunderstood. We tend to imagine it as silence in a room, a break from busy schedules, or peace in the environment around us. But the kind of stillness this devotional prayer guide invites you to discover goes deeper. It is a stillness of the soul, a quiet center within you where God's presence whispers, no matter what noise surrounds you. It's not about escaping the world; it's about finding the sacred space inside you *while* you are in it.

You can be in a crowded street, a bustling workplace, or a chaotic home, and still be deeply connected to God. This stillness isn't the absence of sound. It's the presence of awareness. It's an inward posture of openness, trust, and reverence. It's the soul's ear turned toward heaven, even as life continues its daily rhythm.

I wrote *Divine Whispers Within* to help you recognize and return to that sacred inner stillness. In the chapters that follow, I will guide you through reflections, prayers, and exercises to help you listen more clearly to God's voice that may already be speaking, already be near, already be within.

THE TWO UNIVERSAL QUESTIONS

1. *How does God speak to your inner soul?*
2. *How do you discern God's voice from personal thoughts?*

Those two questions are at the core of what we will discuss. Let's address the first question of how God speaks. Some people find it preposterous or presumptuous to insinuate that God speaks. I am not one of them. God is a living being and living beings communicate with other beings. Even the animal kingdom finds creatures communicating as only they can do. Then why would it be so bizarre that the God who created the creatures, and created humans in His image, would reveal Himself to His creation.

I have found that the problem is people misunderstand how God speaks. You may long to hear from God, imagining His voice as thunderous or unmistakable. But most often, it is a whisper, gentle yet unmistakably divine. And that whisper can come through any number of media. If you are looking and listening, then God is speaking to you. Here are some of the most common ways you can experience God speaking:

1. *Through Scripture*

    God's Word is a living voice. Sometimes a verse you've read many times suddenly comes alive and speaks directly to your situation.

It feels personal, timely, and unmistakably God-breathed. (See 2 Timothy 3:16 - *"All Scripture is God-breathed and is useful for teaching, rebuking, correcting and training in righteousness."*)

2. *Through the Inner Prompting of the Holy Spirit*

    This prompting is often referred to as the "still, small voice," a quiet, inner knowing or nudge that brings both peace and clarity. It may affirm a choice or stir conviction. (See Acts 16:6-7 - *"Paul and his companions traveled throughout the region of Phrygia and Galatia, having been kept by the Holy Spirit from preaching the word in the province of Asia. When they came to the border of Mysia, they tried to enter Bithynia, but the Spirit of Jesus would not allow them to."*) This scripture is an actual example of divine leading and direction.

3. *Through Dreams and Visions*

    Throughout history, God has spoken through dreams, offering guidance, warnings, and spiritual insights. (See Matthew 1:20 - *"But after he had considered this, an angel of the Lord appeared to him in a dream and said, Joseph son of David, do not be afraid to take Mary home as your wife, because what is conceived in her is from the Holy Spirit."* Matthew 2:13 - *"When they had gone, an angel of the Lord appeared to Joseph in a dream. Get up, he said, take the child and his mother and escape to Egypt. Stay there until I tell you, for Herod is going to search for the child to kill him."* Matthew 2:19-20 - *"After Herod died, an angel of the Lord appeared in a dream to Joseph in Egypt, and said, Get up, take the child and his mother and go to the land of Israel, for those who were trying to take the child's life are dead."*) God instructed Joseph in a dream to marry Mary, go to Egypt, and then return to Israel.

4. *Through Nature and Creation*

Creation often awakens us to God's glory and gently whispers His presence (See Psalm 19:1-4 - *"The heavens declare the glory of God; the skies proclaim the work of his hands. Day after day they pour forth speech; night after night they reveal knowledge. They have no speech, they use no words; no sound is heard from them. Yet their voice goes out into all the earth, their words to the ends of the world. In the heavens God has pitched a tent for the sun."*) A walk through the woods, the waves crashing at the shore, or the stars and moon lighting up the night sky all "speak" of

God's existence and majesty.

5. *Through Other People*

   God frequently uses the wise counsel from a friend, an encouraging word from a stranger, or a timely sermon to reveal truth or confirm what's already stirring within you. (See Proverbs 27:17 - *"As iron sharpens iron so one person sharpens another."*)

6. *Through Circumstances*

   Open and closed doors, interruptions, divine delays, and unexpected blessings can all become tools of divine direction when you're listening.

7. *Through Peace or Conviction*

   God's voice often leaves a deep, steady peace even when the message is challenging. Sometimes it brings conviction, a weighty sense of needing to turn, surrender, or obey.

Now let's address the second question of how to distinguish God's voice from the thoughts in your mind. Discerning God's voice can be confusing, especially when your heart, fears, and desires are clamoring for attention at the same time. But spiritual discernment is like tuning a media device; you learn to recognize the signal through experience, Scripture, and prayer. Here are helpful ways to tell when the voice is truly His:

- *It aligns with Scripture.*

  God will never contradict His Word.

If the prompting defies biblical truth, it is not from Him.

- *It brings peace, not pressure.*

  God's whispers are not frantic, manipulative, or fear-driven. They bring peace, even if they challenge you to change or grow. Pressure, anxiety, or a sense of urgency driven by ego are often signs that you need to pause and pray.

- *It is repeated or confirmed.*

  God often repeats His message through Scripture, conversations, circumstances, or even consistent patterns in life. When you see a theme surface again and again, pay attention.

- *It is recognized in silence.*

  Quiet time with God creates space to hear Him. When you slow down through prayer, His tone becomes familiar. Stillness sharpens discernment.

- *It is affirmed by spiritual counsel.*

  Talk with a trusted pastor, mentor, or spiritual friend. Sometimes others can help you distinguish between divine guidance and personal desire.

- *It Bears Good Fruit*

  God's voice leads to transformation. If a whisper produces love, joy, peace, patience, kindness, or humility (See

Galatians 5:22-23 – *"But the fruit of the Spirit is love, joy, peace, forbearance, kindness, goodness, faithfulness, gentleness and self-control. Against such things there is no law."*) You are likely walking in step with the Spirit and "hearing" God's voice when based on the fruit of the Spirit.

AN INVITATION

As you read this devotional prayer guide, don't rush. Take your time. Approach each chapter as a sacred pause. Listen for God not just with your ears, but with your heart. Stillness isn't something you find once; it's something you return to again and again. And in that stillness, you will hear the whisper of God.

INTRODUCTION

During my time teaching technology for the Student, Faculty, and Staff Development Program at the University of Pittsburgh, I met an older, non-traditional student who was returning to school after many years. Surrounded by younger students who seemed more academically and technologically advanced, he confided in me that he felt intimidated and overwhelmed. His fears were not unique. Over the years, I encountered many students who carried similar insecurities about starting over and feeling out of place.

Moved by his vulnerability, I chose to mentor him. Week after week, we met to work through his concerns. Slowly, he began to rebuild his confidence—not only as a student, but as a person with purpose. He later expressed deep gratitude for the time I had invested in him, saying that our connection had reached a level of intimacy because he felt seen, supported, and safe enough to share his personal struggles—including his journey through addiction and recovery.

After listening to the student's comment of appreciation, I asked him a simple question: "Tell me something you know about me, beyond being your mentor."

He paused, thought for a while, and then admitted he couldn't answer. That moment sparked an important realization. I explained that while he had often shared his heart with me, he had never asked about my life outside of being his mentor. True intimacy, I told him, involves *mutual transparency*: a relationship where both parties share, listen, and trust.

That conversation stirred something deeper in me. I began to reflect on my relationship with God:

Have I truly listened to Him, or have I mostly talked?

Do I spend more time making requests than making space?

That "aha moment" inspired me to seek a deeper level of intimacy with God.

First Kings 19:11-13 tells the story of Elijah seeking God during a time of fear and discouragement. God was not found in a mighty wind, an earthquake, or fire but in a "still small voice" or "gentle whisper."

> The LORD said, "Go out and stand on the mountain in the presence of the LORD, for the LORD is about to pass by." Then a great and powerful wind tore the mountains apart and shattered the rocks before the LORD, but the LORD was not in the wind. After the wind there was an earthquake, but the LORD was not in the earthquake. After the earthquake came a fire, but the LORD was not in the fire. And after the fire came a gentle whisper.

When Elijah heard it, he pulled his cloak over his face and went out and stood at the mouth of the cave. Then a voice said to him, "What are you doing here, Elijah?" (NIV).

If you're ready to experience God not just as a distant deity but as a present companion, I encourage you to slow down, be still, and open your heart as you read. This devotional journey will help you tune in to His voice, recognize His presence in your everyday life, and thus deepen your connection to the One who knows you best and loves you most.

Yes, God is still speaking. And He's speaking to *you*. This is your invitation to listen.

Dr. Vernon Franklin
Pittsburgh, PA
September 2025

CHAPTER ONE

BE STILL – GOD IS IN HIS HOLY TEMPLE

In a fast-moving world, your soul longs for stillness. This chapter invites you to pause, quiet your heart, and rediscover what it means to hear God in the silence.

The Bible often refers to the human body as the *temple of God*, emphasizing not only the sacredness of your physical being but also the divine presence that dwells within you. In 1 Corinthians 6:19-20, Paul wrote,

> Do you not know that your bodies are temples of the Holy Spirit, who is in you. . . . You are not your own; you were bought at a price. Therefore, honor God with your bodies.

This verse reminds you that your body is not simply a vessel for physical life but is a sacred space where the Spirit of God resides. Your soul, the most intimate part of your being, is where God speaks in whispers that resonate deeper than any external sound.

Stillness is not just the absence of noise; it is an intentional act of quieting the world around and within you to hear the *Divine Whisper*. It's a moment of reverent pause in worshipful awareness when you become fully present with God. In this stillness, your thoughts, emotions, and spirit are in alignment as God whispers divine truth and revelation. Psalm 37:7 says, "Be still before the Lord and wait patiently for Him." Stillness teaches you to wait—not just with silence, but with anticipation and trust.

My initial realization of this truth came when encountering two extraordinarily sacred moments—one while standing at a busy intersection, and another during a quiet pre-sunrise morning. In both moments, I felt a prompt in my soul to slow down and listen, not with my ears, but with my heart. I heard the whisper: *Be still. God is in His holy temple.*

That inner voice wasn't audible, but it was undeniable. A profound stillness came over me—my mind uncluttered, my emotions calmed, and my soul revitalized. Even amidst the city noise and the early morning quietness before sunrise, I sensed the Holy Presence dwelling within me. And in that stillness, I realized the Divine within me—God was in His holy temple.

Stillness, as explored in this chapter, is more than physical silence; it's a sacred posture of the soul. It's an inner quiet where your spirit becomes attuned to the presence of God, unhindered by external noise, life's demands, or the clutter of constant thought. The world doesn't govern the stillness within you; it comes from recognizing that God, as Habakkuk 2:20 declares, is *"The Lord is in his holy temple: let all the earth keep silence before him."* And 1 Corinthians 6:19 reminds you, *"Do you not know that your bodies are temples of the Holy Spirit, who is in you, whom you have received from God?"* Thus, your body is a dwelling place for the Holy Spirit. He isn't somewhere far off in the distance, He's within you.

Stillness is not about escaping your life but more about immersing yourself in it more deeply but this time with awareness. It's quiet confidence, a sense of spiritual centeredness in which you are not striving, proving, or performing. Stillness isn't solely about maintaining a calm posture during devotional times; instead, it's about quieting your soul at any moment, regardless of what is happening internally or externally. In this sacred place within, God speaks not with thunder or clamor, but with whispers.

In the chapters that follow, you'll gain more clarity on what it means to listen for these *Divine Whispers* and how they often arise in the stillness of your soul. Through testimonies and spiritual exercises, you'll begin to recognize that God's voice isn't far off; it dwells within.

This chapter marks the beginning of your journey inward towards your *sacred space* where God whispers. Maybe you are among the many who have asked, "Does God still speak today?" The answer is yes. He has spoken to men and women throughout history, and He still does—sometimes through Scripture, sometimes through another person, sometimes through quiet revelations that awaken something deep within. He speaks in moments of joy, in pain, in questions, and even in silence.

You don't need to apply a formula or create the perfect atmosphere. God knows how to reach you—because He created you. Your spiritual ear may already be hearing His voice; you just may not have realized it.

So, be still and open your heart. God is in His holy temple and His whispers will come at His appointed time.

CHAPTER SUMMARY

This chapter introduced the biblical foundation of stillness as a spiritual posture—one that invites you to rest, wait, and listen for God's voice within your soul. Drawing from verses like Psalm 46:10 and Exodus 14:14, it emphasized that stillness is not simply the absence of noise but a sacred awareness of God's presence within His holy temple—your inner being. In a world full of noise and distractions, God calls you to quiet the chaos, embrace silence, and receive His revelation in your sacred space.

DEVOTIONAL PRAYER GUIDE EXERCISE

CHAPTER ONE:

BE STILL – GOD IS IN HIS HOLY TEMPLE

Theme: Practicing Sacred Stillness

1. Reflection Journal Prompt:
Recall a moment when you felt still mentally, emotionally, or spiritually.

- What was happening around you?
- What did you feel at that moment?
- Did you sense God's presence?

Write about that experience and what it taught you about stillness.

2. Sacred Stillness Practice:
Find a quiet space. Sit in silence for 5–10 minutes with no distractions. As you breathe deeply, think about Psalm 46:10, "Be still and know that I am God." Let your soul settle. Let the silence become sacred.

3. Scripture Meditation:

> *Lamentations 3:26 – "It is good to wait quietly for the salvation of the LORD."*
>
> *Exodus 14:14 – "The Lord will fight for you; you need only to be still."*
>
> *Psalm 37:7 – "Be still before the Lord and wait patiently for Him."*

4. Personal Stillness Ritual:
Establish a time this week when you will pause from your routine. There will be no phone or talking just being still before God. Consider making this a weekly habit of sacred surrender and listening.

CLOSING PRAYER

Lord, help me slow down and silence the noise within and around me. Teach me to be still, not just with my body, but with my soul. Let Your presence fill the sacred space within me. In the stillness, may I hear Your voice and know that You are God. Amen.

CHAPTER TWO
YOUR SPIRITUAL UMBILICAL CORD

You are not disconnected or forgotten. Like a child in the womb, your soul is connected to God through a sacred lifeline. This chapter reminds you that divine nourishment and guidance are always within reach.

Amid life's chaos created by a convergence of routines, emergencies, work commitments, family obligations, crises, and deadlines, it can be difficult to find a moment of peace. Yet Scripture reminds us to "be still." Zechariah 2:13 says, *"Be still before the LORD, all mankind, because he has roused himself from his holy dwelling."* and Exodus 14:14 declares, *"The Lord will fight for you; you need only to be still."* These verses emphasize not just God's power, but also the trust and surrender we are called to embrace, especially during difficult times.

Stillness isn't just the absence of noise or movement. True stillness reaches beyond the body and mind; it is a quieting of the heart and soul. It is the deep assurance that, even when life is spinning fast, you can rest in God's sovereignty. It is the peace that comes not from having control but from letting go and trusting the One who holds it all.

So how do you prioritize stillness when everything around you seems urgent? Urgent tasks demand your immediate attention, while important tasks beckon that align with your long-term values and purpose. Stillness is both urgent and important. It isn't optional, it's foundational. It brings clarity and perspective before you act, respond, or decide.

Many people go through life unaware of the essence and purpose of their soul. The soul is more than a theological concept; it is your true self, the innermost part of your being that connects directly to God. When God breathed life into humanity, we became living souls. That breath was not just biological, it was spiritual. It gave birth to your authenticity which empowers you to embrace your true self as God lovingly created you.

Think of your soul as a spiritual umbilical cord connecting you to your Creator. Just as a baby receives life-sustaining nutrients through a physical cord in the womb, your soul receives divine nourishment from God. The baby's umbilical cord includes one vein bringing in nutrients and two arteries removing waste, which reveals something significant. God not only supplies you with life and purpose, but He also helps cleanse and release the emotional and spiritual toxins you accumulate.

Through this sacred cord, God supplies your soul with insight, purpose, comfort, and wisdom. He invites you into a relationship at the core of your being. And just like a mother never stops nurturing her child, God never stops reaching out to you. *But do you hear Him?*

Many people ask whether God speaks audibly. The better question than does God speak is, *"Are you listening as God has chosen to reveal Himself to you?"* God is omniscient. He communicates in the way you can receive Him most clearly. Whether through voice, conscience, dreams, intuition, emotion, intellect, or a spiritual nudge, God knows how to get your attention.

Have you ever been moved by a sermon or speech? Stilled by the majesty of nature? Encouraged by a Scripture verse or a line in a book? That stirring in your soul producing warmth, clarity, or conviction is a whisper from God. He speaks through moments that move you, reminding you of

His presence and your purpose. Your soul is sacred ground and a private sanctuary reserved solely for fellowship with God. He is your true soulmate, the one who nourishes your soul like no other.

Yet sometimes your soul can become like a warehouse and not a home, cluttered with unresolved emotions, residue from unhealthy relationships, and worldly distractions. When overcrowded, your sacred space becomes so noisy that there's no way to hear God's still, small voice. *If that's the case, it's time to clean house.*

Eliminate the clutter. Let go of the distractions. Make space within your soul to hear clearly again—or maybe for the first time. As you abide with God, your soul will not only find peace, but it will also grow, expand, and thrive in ways beyond what you thought possible.

CHAPTER SUMMARY

In this chapter, we explored the metaphor of the soul as a spiritual umbilical cord, a sacred lifeline that connects you to God. Just as a baby receives nourishment and releases waste through this cord, your soul receives divine wisdom and sheds spiritual toxins through ongoing fellowship with God. Stillness, therefore, is not passive; it's an act of prioritizing a relationship with your Creator.

By embracing spiritual stillness, cleaning out life's clutter, and listening for God's voice, you begin to experience life with greater clarity and purpose that's fully aligned with the One who sustains your soul.

DEVOTIONAL PRAYER GUIDE EXERCISE

CHAPTER TWO:

YOUR SPIRITUAL UMBILICAL CORD

Theme: Tuning In to Your Divine Whispers

1. Reflection Journal Prompt:
Take ten minutes today to reflect on this question: *What worldly or situational "clutter" is crowding my soul right now?* Write down anything, such as unresolved tension, worry, guilt, and distractions that may be blocking your ability to feel close to God.

2. Sacred Listening Moment:
Find a quiet space. Close your eyes. Take three deep breaths. As you breathe, imagine God's presence flowing through your soul cleansing, nourishing, and comforting. Whisper this prayer:

> *"God, clear the noise. I want to hear You. Speak to me in a way I understand. Amen."*

3. Scripture Meditation:
Read and meditate on one of the following:

- Psalm 131:2 – *"But I have calmed and quieted myself, I am like a weaned child with its mother; like a weaned child I am content."*

- Philippians 4:6-7 – *"Do not be anxious about anything, but in every situation, by prayer and petition, with thanksgiving, present your requests to God. And the peace of God, which transcends all understanding, will guard your hearts and your minds in Christ Jesus."*
- Lamentations 3:26 – *"It is good to wait quietly for the salvation of the LORD."*

4. Soul Decluttering Action Step:

Reflect on the metaphor of the umbilical cord. What do you need to nourish your soul this week? Choose one thing to release: an unnecessary obligation, a toxic thought pattern, or a draining relationship. Whatever it is, replace it with intentional time alone with God.

CLOSING PRAYER

God, thank You for the divine connection between us, which is the sacred lifeline that began when You breathed life into my soul. Remind me that I am never disconnected from You. Even in moments of doubt or struggle, help me feel the steady flow of Your love and guidance. May I grow deeper in trust, fed by Your presence and sustained by Your divine whispers. Amen.

CHAPTER THREE

SACRED PLACE

Your soul has an inner sanctuary, a space reserved for God alone. In this chapter, you'll learn how to protect that space and recognize the importance of keeping God at the center of your life.

In the midst of a noisy world full of demands, distractions, and constant motion, there is a place deep within you that remains untouched. It is not a physical location or a space that can be seen with the eye, but a sacred inner sanctuary of your soul that belongs to God alone. It is in this space that you find true rest, clarity, and communion.

This chapter invites you to slow down and recognize that the presence of God isn't something you need to chase. He is already near. In fact, He dwells within you. Your sacred place is not somewhere you visit occasionally during crisis or quiet times. It is a place of continuous relationship, a holy dwelling place within your soul.

Externally you are surrounded by relationships; some casual, some meaningful, and a few deeply personal. A helpful way to understand these connections is through the concentric circle model, a visual framework that illustrates relational closeness based on trust and intimacy:

- Outer Circle: These are acquaintances, coworkers, casual friends, or social media contacts. Their knowledge of you is surface-level, and access to your inner life is limited.

- Intermediate Circle: This includes close friends, family, or mentors who know more about you, share moments of your life, and offer emotional support, but still reside outside your inner circle.

- Inner Circle: These are the few who have walked beside you in joy and pain, those with whom you've shared your deepest stories and who have earned your trust over time.

Notice the following Typical Relational Model and how each circle gets smaller as the relationships become closer. Thus, the smallest circle is where you develop intimate relationships, feeling closeness and emotionally connected and supported.

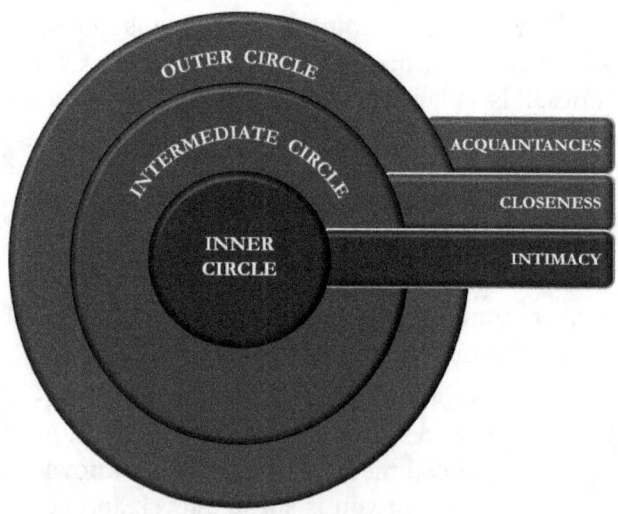

Figure 1: Typical Relational Model

A variation of the *typical relational model* can be found in a wide range of applications used in educational strategies, along with scientific and business models. They represent a visual way to organize information, explore relationships, and understand systems.

Beyond the *Typical Relational Model* is something even more profound, something not shared in its external relationship model. The Divine Relational Model represents both your external relationships and your internal relationship (a place reserved for God alone).

The following Divine Relational Model consists of an additional smaller inner circle that represents your soul. This relational circle is the smallest circle within the concentric circles—the most intimate relationship of all; the *Sacred Place* for you and God. The other circles are not part of your being but represent external relationships.

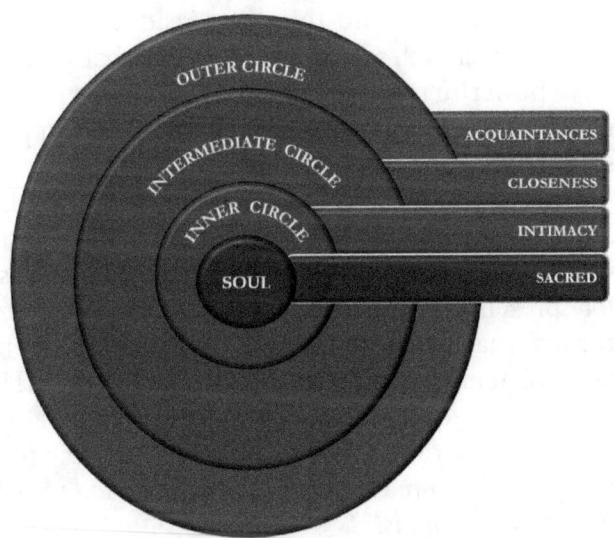

Figure 2: Divine Relational Model

The smallest circle represents your spirit,

the inner sanctuary where God dwells, breathed life, and established His divine connection to your soul. As I noted in previous chapters, God speaks in numerous ways internally and externally. Your soul is the most intimate and sacred place where *Divine Whispers* and confirmation of external communications are experienced.

Within the very center of your being where all your emotions, thoughts, and experiences exist is your *Sacred Place*. This is the innermost circle of the Divine Relational Model. It is a spiritual chamber not accessible to any external relationship, not even those closest to you. It is the dwelling place of God's Spirit; the breath of life He placed within you when He created you in His image.

As Habakkuk 2:20 declares, *"The Lord is in His holy temple; let all the earth keep silence before Him."* I've often heard this verse read as a call to worship in church services. But beyond that setting, it is a powerful reminder to *quiet your soul* in recognition of God's presence. Worship begins when you stop striving and start listening.

This inner temple is holy ground. Just as the ancient Israelites carried the portable tabernacle through the wilderness and experienced God's visible presence in the cloud and fire, you now carry the tabernacle within you. God no longer resides in tents or temples made by human hands; thus, He lives within you. The Apostle Paul personalizes this truth in 1 Corinthians 3:16: *"Don't you know that you yourselves are God's temple and that God's Spirit dwells in your midst?"*

God chose to dwell within your sacred space not only to comfort you, but to communicate with you. This is where the *Divine Whisper* is clearest. It's not always a loud declaration or miraculous sign. Most often, it is a quiet impression, a gentle nudge, a wordless knowing that brings peace and conviction.

Sacred Stillness is where worship begins and guidance flows. Stillness in this context is not the absence of sound but the presence of spiritual awareness. It is a stillness of the soul, a posture that is open, alert, and undistracted. It means quieting the internal chatter, pausing the urgency of your to-do list, and making space to listen.

Sometimes, the silence may feel unbearable, especially when you're waiting for an answer or facing uncertainty. In these moments, you might be tempted to fill the sacred space with activity, noise, advice, or comfort from others in your relational circles. While those external relationships are valuable, they are not meant to take God's place. Substituting divine communion with human validation or external busyness leaves you spiritually malnourished. It is like offering fast food to a soul created for a banquet of glory.

Your sacred place must be guarded, nurtured, and respected. It is not a side room for occasional visits but a sanctuary of ongoing relationship. It is the only place where you are fully known and unconditionally loved. And it is the only place where your purpose is not just discovered but revealed.

Before you move on to the chapter summary, reflect on these questions:

- Have you been treating your sacred place as a sanctuary or a storage room?
- What voices or distractions tend to invade that space?

- What would it look like to protect it, honor it, and dwell with God there more consistently?

CHAPTER SUMMARY

This chapter revealed that your most intimate relationship is not with external relationships but with God, who dwells in the sacred center of your soul. Using the Divine Relational Model, you learned how your relationships move from distant to close, but your spirit holds a place reserved for God alone.

As you honor this sacred place, you awaken to the reality that God is not far off. He is within. He whispers not to your ears, but to your soul. And through this whisper, He leads you, loves you, and reveals your identity and purpose.

DEVOTIONAL PRAYER GUIDE EXERCISE

CHAPTER THREE: SACRED PLACE

Theme: Guard Your Sacred Space

1. Reflection Journal Prompt:
Draw three concentric circles on a page. Label them **Outer**, **Intermediate**, and **Inner Circle**. Now reflect on this question: *Who or what have I allowed into my sacred center that might be clouding my ability to hear God?* Write down anything you may need to release to reclaim your holy space.

2. Stillness Practice:
Set aside five minutes today. Sit quietly and slowly whisper this prayer:
"God, I honor You in the holy temple of my soul. Let everything else be silent so I may hear only You."
Visualize your sacred place like the center of a tabernacle—calm, lit by divine fire, free of distractions.

3. Scripture Meditation:

- Habakkuk 2:20 – *"The Lord is in his holy temple; let all the earth be silent before him."*
- 1 Corinthians 3:16-17 – *"Don't you know that you yourselves are God's temple and that God's Spirit dwells in your midst? If anyone destroys God's temple, God will destroy that person;*

for God's temple is sacred, and you together are that temple."

- Psalm 27:14 – *"Wait for the Lord; be strong and take heart and wait for the Lord."*

4. Sacred Space Commitment:
Choose one boundary you can set this week to protect your soul's stillness. Whether it's limiting social media, saying no to an unnecessary commitment, or unplugging for one hour daily, do it intentionally as an act of reverence.

CLOSING PRAYER

Lord, You are the center of my soul, the sacred place where only You belong. Help me protect this holy space from the clutter of distractions, burdens, and misplaced loyalties. Teach me to honor the temple within and to guard it as the dwelling place of Your presence. May I keep You at the center and listen closely for Your voice. Amen.

CHAPTER FOUR

AN AWAKENING

Sometimes, the most profound encounters with God happen when you least expect it. This chapter explores how divine whispers can speak to you in the middle of ordinary life's routines.

The first time I sensed something different in my prayer life was during the early years of my career. A regular devotional time had always been an essential part of my spiritual journey. Mornings were especially meaningful because my mind felt refreshed, and I could reflect clearly on my schedule, responsibilities, and life situations. This quiet space became the perfect setting for intercessory prayer.

I developed a rhythm: certain days were dedicated to praying for specific people, the community, my workplace, various ministries, and national/global situations. My devotional practice included reading Scripture, journaling my thoughts and requests, and noting answered prayers. Over time, these morning devotions became routine. There were moments when they began to feel like a duty. Have you ever felt like that, like your devotional time was just another item on your to-do list?

The God of the universe who is limitless in creativity is never ordinary. But sometimes, our perception of God can become too small, shaped by habit, routine, and culture. And when that happens, our time with Him can become just that—*routine*.

One afternoon, my understanding of devotion expanded in a way I didn't expect. I had just finished lunch and was walking back to my office on a college campus. The streets were alive with movement as cars rushed by and students hurried to class, their conversations swirling in the air. As I waited at the intersection for the light to change, suddenly a peaceful presence descended over me. Amid the noise and motion, I experienced a moment of divine stillness.

I noticed the gentle breeze and the warmth of sunlight on my face. Looking up at the sky, in that moment I felt completely connected to God, to the universe, and to something greater than myself. I didn't pray. I didn't recite any Scripture. I didn't need to. I simply stood still, acutely aware that *God was speaking directly to my soul* through the wind, the sky, and the stillness within.

This moment on a busy street corner was a personal turning point. It taught me that *devotion* is not confined to a morning schedule or a quiet corner reading a Bible. God's voice isn't limited to my expectations of when or how He will speak.

Since that experience, there have been other moments that replicated this same type of spiritual awakening. Another came while I sat in a doctor's office with an unexpected illness. Another occurred after an early morning jog. In both instances, I felt a similar nudge that God was reaching out beyond the limits of my routine, whispering assurance, peace, and love into my being.

Each of these encounters revealed something profound: *God is always near*, not just during times of worship and devotion, but in every part of life. These moments of *awakening* taught me to pay attention, to expect the sacred in the ordinary, and to listen for the *Divine Whispers* that connect my soul to God's presence. This awakening transformed my relationship with God. No longer was our conversation one-sided. I became more open, aware, and eager to engage in moments of sacred exchange, no matter where I was or what I was doing.

CHAPTER SUMMARY

This chapter invited you to reflect on how God may be speaking to you outside the boundaries of traditional devotion. God can communicate in unexpected encounters, such as in a crowd or during a doctor's visit, emphasizing that *He is not confined to ritual.* He is always speaking, always near, and always seeking to awaken you to a deeper connection.

Awakening to the *Divine Whispers Within* opens you to an intimate, ongoing relationship with God that is not based on routine, but on presence—both His and yours. This chapter reminded you that *spiritual sensitivity* can be cultivated in unlikely moments when you are still, aware, and open to divine interruption.

DEVOTIONAL PRAYER GUIDE EXERCISE

CHAPTER FOUR: AN AWAKENING

Theme: Awaken to the Sacred in the Ordinary

1. Reflection Journal Prompt
Think back to a time when you felt a sudden sense of peace, awe, or clarity in an unexpected place.

- Where were you?
- What were you doing?
- How did it feel?
- Could it have been God whispering to your soul?

Write about that moment and what it might have been revealing to you.

2. Awareness Practice
Set an intention today to become aware of God's presence outside your normal devotion time. Whisper this prayer at the start of your day: *"God, awaken me to Your presence, even in the unexpected."* Then throughout the day, pause for 15 seconds to breathe, observe your surroundings, and quiet your soul.

3. Scripture Meditation
- Psalm 139:7-10 – *"Where can I go from Your Spirit?"*
- Isaiah 30:21 – *" Whether you*

> *turn to the right or to the left, your ears will hear a voice behind you, saying, 'This is the way; walk in it'."*

- John 10:27 – *"My sheep listen to my voice; I know them, and they follow me."*

4. Active Listening Walk

Take a 10-minute walk, preferably outdoors (or sit outside). As you walk, ask: *God, what are You saying to me in this moment?* Feel the wind, observe the sky, the people, the stillness, and listen with your soul.

CLOSING PRAYER

God, awaken me to Your presence in the everyday moments of life. Open my eyes to see You, even in the ordinary. Teach me to be fully present so I don't miss the subtle ways You reveal Yourself. Let Your whispers awaken my soul with love, assurance, and purpose. Amen.

CHAPTER FIVE
DIVINE WHISPERS

Have you ever felt a nudge, a prompt, or a sudden peace that seemed to be a divine intervention? This chapter reveals how Divine Whispers can get your attention during life's daily routines.

Have you ever felt a nudge from within, a sudden prompt about how to handle a situation, a warning about something on the horizon, or a gentle reminder to reach out to someone? Perhaps you've been inspired by a new idea or overwhelmed by a sense of peace that seemed to arrive out of nowhere. These moments may be answers to a question many ask: *Can God speak to me? And if so, how?*

The truth is, *God still speaks*. He has never stopped communicating to and through His creation since the beginning when He first spoke to Adam and Eve in the Garden. Sometimes, God's voice comes in the form of a mental prompting. You may wonder, *where did that thought come from? Was it from God?* While not every thought is divinely inspired, when you are actively seeking a relationship with God, you can trust that He will speak and that His voice will become more familiar over time.

Scripture assures us with the words of Jesus in John 10:27, *"My sheep hear my voice, and I know them, and they follow me."* Jesus identifies Himself as the Good Shepherd who knows His sheep, and whose sheep recognize His voice. And then He said in John 15:4, *"Abide in me, and I in you."* This mutual abiding creates an intimate connection where divine whispers become recognizable.

God's promptings can occur at any time, not just during prayer or devotions. As your relationship with Him grows, you will begin to hear these *Divine Whispers* during everyday life. Let me share with you a few moments from my own journey where God's voice broke through in powerful and unexpected ways.

MORNING WALK

Early in my career, I faced significant financial challenges. My salary didn't cover all my basic needs, forcing me into a cycle of decreasing and rotating payments from one bill to pay another. The stress was constant. Despite seeking advice on debt relief, I found no lasting solution.

One morning, while walking before work and wrestling with frustration, I suddenly heard a clear, gentle whisper in my spirit: "Be still." Those words calmed me. I remembered Psalm 46:10: "Be still, and know that I am God." Though no immediate solution appeared, I was filled with peace and hope.

Later, another quiet confirmation came during a 3:30 a.m. walk in darkness. As birds began to sing, I knew dawn was near. That simple reminder from nature reassured me: *The sun is rising. Things will change.*

WHILE DRIVING

On another difficult morning, a driver cut me off and then made a rude gesture. I was enraged and impulsively followed them, determined to confront them at the next light. When we pulled up side by side, both our windows rolled down, and before I could speak, the driver said, "God bless you."

Stunned and speechless, I rolled up my window and drove away.

As I processed what had just happened, a

whisper echoed in my heart: "That was so unlike you. What prompted you to do such a thing?" In that moment, I realized I was carrying more than just road rage—I was burdened by unspoken stress from personal, work, and church challenges.

That Divine Whisper didn't just correct me, it led me to healing. I made an appointment with a counselor that very day.

SHOPPING AT THE GROCERY STORE

After a discouraging day, I felt overwhelmed by low self-esteem. My personal and professional life didn't feel aligned with my purpose. Stopping at a grocery store on the way home, I kept my head down, just trying to get through the evening.

As I walked down an aisle, a stranger passed me and said, "Pardon me, sir. I don't mean to bother you, I just want you to know, I see something good in you." And just like that, he was gone. I turned to respond, but he had vanished. I stood there stunned.

Then I heard the Divine Whisper: "I love you." The *Divine Whisper* reminded me that I was seen, valued, and deeply loved by God even when I didn't feel it.

WORKPLACE OFFICE

As time passed in my career, I began to feel stagnant despite current and past accomplishments. I longed for something new, but I wasn't sure what. In prayer, I asked, *"Where do I go from here, God?"*

The *Divine Whispers* nudged me to return to school, yet I resisted. I had already earned multiple degrees and vowed I was finished with formal education. The prompting remained in my spirit; thus, I decided to pursue professional development.

Seeking counsel from trusted spiritual advisors, both felt my educational endeavor wasn't necessary, and I even received a rejection from a doctoral program. Still, the inner prompting remained. Eventually, a new hybrid doctoral program opened at the university where I worked, made affordable because of my employee benefits. I was accepted, completed the program, and soon after, new opportunities opened. God's whispers had seen further down the road than I ever could.

HOME OFFICE

Before starting my doctoral program, I turned my spare bedroom into a home office. One day, while sitting at the desk, I felt a wave of anxiety about the journey ahead. Looking out the window, I heard a gentle whisper: *"After graduation, you will publish books."* That whisper of encouragement came from a sovereign God who knows the future. I graduated successfully, and this devotional book is now my third publication.

In every stage of my life from despair to growth, *Divine Whispers Within* guided me, rebuked me, encouraged me, and prepared me for what was to come.

God is speaking. Are you listening?

CHAPTER SUMMARY

This chapter highlighted the diverse ways God speaks through promptings in daily life with examples from my own life while walking, driving, shopping, and working. These *Divine Whispers* are not just emotional impressions, but spiritual messages meant to guide, affirm, correct, and direct. As your relationship with God deepens, you will recognize these promptings as divine, tailor-made communications from the One who knows you best.

The lesson is simple but profound: *God will speak—you must quiet your soul enough to listen.*

DEVOTIONAL PRAYER GUIDE EXERCISE

CHAPTER FIVE: DIVINE WHISPERS

Theme: Recognizing Your Divine Whispers

1. Reflection Journal Prompt
Write about a moment when you sensed an inner prompting or sudden thought that later proved meaningful.
- What happened?
- How did it feel?
- Do you believe it was a *Divine Whisper*? Why or why not?

2. Whisper Awareness Practice
Throughout this week, pause at least once each day and pray, *"God, help me recognize Your voice in my everyday life."* Keep a small notepad or use a phone note to record any thoughts or nudges that stand out.

3. Scripture Meditation
- Zechariah 2:13 – *"Be still before the LORD, all mankind, because he has roused himself from his holy dwelling."*
- Lamentations 3:26 – *"It is good to wait quietly for the salvation of the LORD"*.
- Psalm 37:7 – *"Be still before the LORD and wait patiently for him;*

> *do not fret when people succeed in their ways, when they carry out their wicked schemes."*

4. Divine Whispers Mapping
Using five areas (walking, driving, shopping, working at job, living at home), create a chart or mind map of moments where you might be most open to hearing God's voice. This will help increase awareness and expectation in everyday routines.

CLOSING PRAYER.

Lord, help me quiet the noise around me so I can recognize Your Divine Whispers. Tune my heart to hear You when You speak whether through a thought, a person, or a moment of peace. Teach me to trust Your voice and respond with faith, even when the whisper is gentle and unexpected. Amen.

CHAPTER SIX

ACTS TOWARD RELATIONSHIP

God desires a relationship not just ritual. In this chapter, you'll explore four spiritual acts that make space for Divine Whispers and deepen your daily connection with the Divine.

My life's journey has provided me with countless learning experiences through family, church, community, and my professional career. In each of these areas, I have felt God's presence, prompting, and influence. I refer to these divine encounters as the *Divine Whispers Within*.

As discussed in previous chapters, God desires a relationship with you, and to that end has already established a means of communication with you. Yet many people go through life unsure of what it means to have a personal relationship with the Supreme Being—the Creator of the universe. God's infinite nature and divine transcendence can feel overwhelming, even intimidating. It's hard to grasp how someone so powerful could want something so intimate with people like you and me.

And yet, *God is relational by nature*, and He created you as a relational being in His image. When you stop to consider that, everything in creation is interconnected. Relationships are woven into the fabric of the universe, and you were made in God's image and are part of that divine tapestry. You were created as a sacred temple for God to dwell in, and from the moment He breathed life into you, His whispers have echoed within your soul.

You were created *for relationship,* and you already possess the capacity to connect with God. To nurture this divine relationship and tune your heart to hear His whispers, there are *four acts of relational posture* that you can embrace: *Awareness,*

Presence, Anticipation, and Revelation that are illustrated below.

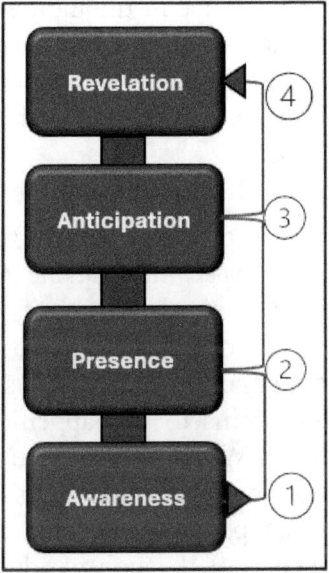

Figure 3: Four Acts of Relational Posture

1. Awareness

The first act is becoming aware of the sacred space within *your soul*. It is in this space that God breathed life into you. This breath, this divine spark, is your living connection to your Creator. Developing awareness of your soul helps you remember that God is not far off. He is already near, residing within your temple, waiting to communicate with you.

2. Presence

Once you are aware of your sacred space, the next act is *being present* in it. Our world is fast-paced, noisy, and filled with constant distractions.

Being present means choosing stillness. It means pausing to focus inward, quieting your surroundings, and finding peace in the moment. It's also in this presence that feelings of loneliness can be felt. You are not alone. You are simply being invited to a deeper intimacy, where God's whispers can be heard more clearly.

3. Anticipation

When you practice presence, your soul begins to wait with *expectation*. *Divine Whispers* don't always come on demand. Sometimes, you may experience quiet seasons, days or weeks without a divine prompt. Remain faithful in the stillness. Even when nothing seems to be happening, trust that God is with you. Waiting on Him in sacred anticipation is an act of faith and love. As in any meaningful relationship, sometimes the greatest connection happens not through words, but through shared stillness.

4. Revelation

Over time, as your soul grows comfortable in solitude and becomes attuned to God's rhythm, you will begin to experience *revelation*. *Divine Whispers* will come—not frequently, but when they do, they're always inspirational. These moments of divine insight and clarity bring encouragement, instruction, and understanding specific to your journey. And because they come from God Himself, they resonate deeply within your spirit.

These four acts are not rituals, they are *relational postures* that help you approach God with openness and trust. By becoming more comfortable functioning within your sacred inner space, you give God permission to meet you there. And when

He does, it is transformational.

In this intimate space, your soul meets its *true soulmate—God Himself*. He will guide your growth, offer you wisdom, and help you make sense of your life's journey. Through His *Divine Whispers Within*, you are never walking alone.

CHAPTER SUMMARY

In this chapter, we explored four key acts that deepen your relationship with God and attune your soul to hear His *Divine Whispers*: Awareness, Presence, Anticipation, and Revelation. These are not religious duties but spiritual movements of the heart. They create sacred posture and space where God's voice can be heard with clarity and assurance.

God, your eternal soulmate, desires an intimate relationship with you. When you intentionally engage in these four postures, your soul becomes more sensitive, more connected, and more open to the divine conversation already happening within you.

DEVOTIONAL PRAYER GUIDE EXERCISE

CHAPTER SIX:

ACTS OF RELATIONAL POSTURE

Theme: Engaging the Four Acts

1. Reflection Journal Prompt:
Which of the four acts—Awareness, Presence, Anticipation, or Revelation—do you feel most connected to right now? Which one do you struggle with the most? Write a paragraph reflecting on how that act is showing up (or missing) in your spiritual life.

2. Four-Day Sacred Practice:
Dedicate the next four days to focusing on one act per day:

- **Day 1 – Awareness:**

    Find a quiet space and reflect on the fact that your soul is sacred and designed for connection with God. Whisper: *"I am aware of Your presence in me."*

- **Day 2 – Presence:**

    Practice 5–10 minutes of silence today. No asking. No talking. Just being still and focusing on God's nearness.

- **Day 3 – Anticipation:**

Start the day by praying: *"God, I am ready for Your whisper whenever and however You choose."* Wait in peace, even if nothing happens.

- **Day 4 – Revelation:**

  Revisit your journal. Did anything stand out? Did you sense a shift in your emotions, thoughts, or peace? Write down anything that feels like a whisper.

3. Scripture Meditation:

- Psalm 130:5 – *"I wait for the Lord, my whole being waits, and in His word I put my hope."*
- Psalm 131:2 – *"But I have calmed and quieted myself, I am like a weaned child with its mother; like a weaned child I am content."*
- Romans 8:16 – *"The Spirit himself testifies with our spirit that we are God's children."*

4. Commitment Prayer:

End your devotional time with this short prayer:

"God, thank You for desiring relationship with me. Help me to walk daily in awareness, be present in Your peace, wait with anticipation, and receive Your revelation. Whisper into my soul and let me respond with love. Amen."

CLOSING PRAYER

God, thank You for desiring a relationship with me. Help me walk in daily awareness of Your presence, be still enough to notice Your whispers, and wait with anticipation for what You want to reveal. Let my soul become a sanctuary where revelation flows from intimacy, not effort. Draw me closer as I draw near to You. Amen.

CHAPTER SEVEN

WHEN DIVINE WHISPERS REVEAL UR-NIQUE PURPOSE

Have you ever sensed that there is something more, something deeper, waiting to be revealed about your life? Listen for the sacred whisper and allow God to direct you toward a life of deeper meaning and greater impact.

This chapter links *Divine Whispers Within* to my previous book on *UR-Nique Purpose: Three A's to Authenticity*. This will help you address the specific situation of listening for *Divine Whispers Within* that will aid you in discovering your life's purpose. My *UR-Nique Purpose* book provides practical step-by-step assessment tools to the discovery of your authentic purpose. This book can be purchased by visiting my website: http://www.franklinconsultingandtrainings.com.

In this chapter, I will guide you inward to your sacred space where you can hear God's whisper based on the principles you have read in this devotional prayer guide. You were created by God with purpose for a meaningful mission in life. So, who is better to tell you about your purpose than God your creator?

Your purpose is not something you must create from scratch, but something already embedded in your soul, waiting to be revealed through divine stillness. When God's whisper reveals your *UR-Nique purpose*, it awakens a sense that you were born to make a difference in the world in a way that only you can.

Often, people look outward to find meaning, measuring their lives by accomplishments, status, or comparison. Yet God's whisper is different. It does not shout or compete. It invites. It speaks within your *Sacred Space* where your soul and God's presence meet. There your essence is affirmed, and the seeds of your purpose begin to bloom.

Throughout Scripture, God met individuals with a whisper that revealed direction and destiny. Moses heard God's call from a burning bush in the wilderness. Joseph heard Him in the form of two dreams. David through the visit of a prophet. Elijah heard it not in the earthquake or fire but in a gentle whisper. Mary received purpose in a quiet encounter with the angel. These divine whispers were not loud, but they were often subtle but life changing nevertheless.

Your life is no different. The whisper of God brings alignment between your passion, gifts, life experiences, and calling. It helps you see how your purpose is not only about what you do, but about who you are and how you serve the world with love.

When you tune into the sacred stillness and respond to God's voice, you move from wandering to walking with intentionality. You begin to live out your UR-Nique purpose with clarity and courage, knowing that your life is a divine response to a holy calling.

CHAPTER SUMMARY

When divine whispers reveals your UR-Nique purpose, it discloses your identity, ignites your calling, and aligns your life with divine intent. This chapter invites you to stop striving and start listening, allowing the stillness within to connect you with the God who created you with purpose. As you become more aware of God's whisper, you will uncover a deeper sense of direction and mission.

DEVOTIONAL PRAYER GUIDE EXERCISE

CHAPTER SEVEN: WHEN GOD'S WHISPER REVEALS UNIQUE PURPOSE

Theme: Divine Purpose Reflection

1. Quiet Your Soul (5–10 minutes):
Find a quiet space. Close your eyes. Take slow, deep breaths. Invite God into your Sacred Space by saying, "Speak Lord, I'm listening."

2. Reflective Writing Prompt:
Journal your responses to the following:

- What inner nudges or whispers have I recently sensed but ignored?
- How have my passions, struggles, or talents been pointing me toward purpose?
- Where in my life do I feel God's gentle call to serve or make a difference?

3. Write what this reflection means to you personally in this season.

CLOSING PRAYER

Lord, I desire to live the life You created me for. Tune my heart to Your whisper. Reveal my purpose. Give me the courage to walk in it, even when I feel uncertain. Let my life echo Your love.

CONCLUSION

THE GOD WHO WHISPERS

It was the *Divine Whisper of God* that spoke the universe into existence. His voice brought forth the beauty of creation and continues to echo through all He has made. Wherever God's whispers resonate, they leave behind trails of love, creativity, and divine revelation.

From the beginning, God has desired relationship with His creation. This longing is seen throughout history in the beauty of nature, in the lives of humanity, and throughout the pages of Scripture. In the Old Testament, God instructed His people to build the Tabernacle, saying, "Let them make Me a sanctuary, that I may dwell among them" (Exodus 25:8). In the New Testament, His desire becomes even more intimate as stated by Paul: "We are the temple of the living God" (2 Corinthians 6:16).

God no longer dwells in tents or temples made by human hands; *He dwells within you.* When He breathed life into your soul, He created a sacred space designed for divine communion. Your soul is now His temple, the place where *Divine Whispers* reside. And even in times when you feel alone or distant from His voice, know this: *His presence has never left your sacred space.*

This holy inner sanctuary was never meant for worldly clutter, temporary fixes, or superficial joy. It belongs solely to the One who gave you life. *Divine Whispers* transcend religious routines and human understanding that go beyond doctrine, cultural noise, or even personal expectations. They cut through confusion and speak directly to the soul.

Consider the stories of Job and Paul who encountered *divine revelation* that exceeded the answers they expected. Instead, they received transformative whispers:

- Job, after losing everything, was surrounded by the unsympathetic logic of friends and the weight of grief. But God's response wasn't a logical explanation but rather a concise, powerful whisper: *"Where were you when I laid the earth's foundation?"* (Job 38). God revealed His grandeur, shifting Job's perspective from despair to awe.

- Paul, tormented by a "thorn in the flesh," pleaded for relief. Instead, God whispered, *"My grace is sufficient for you, for My power is made perfect in weakness"* (2 Corinthians 12:9). Rather than the removal of his thorn, Paul received strength, purpose, and revelation.

In both cases, God's whispers elevated them

above their circumstances and drew them closer to Him.

So, what about you? What burden weighs heavy on your heart? What question lingers unanswered? What personal struggle consumes your thoughts? Take them to your sacred place, your soul where human logic fades and *Divine Whispers bring divine clarity: "The Lord is in His holy temple; let all the earth keep silence before Him"* (Habakkuk 2:20). In the stillness of your soul, God is speaking. *Be aware. Be present. Anticipate. Then receive revelation.*

> You are not alone.
> You are His temple.
> And He is whispering still.

EPILOGUE

LIVING IN SACRED RHYTHM

Your relationship with God is not just a part of your life, it is the *rhythm* that shapes your journey. It is the sacred space within you—your soul where your thoughts, experiences, prayers, and questions meet God's presence in divine conversation.

Throughout this devotional, you've been invited to *still your soul,* listen with intention, and recognize God's *Divine Whispers Within*—whispers of love, wisdom, correction, and encouragement. These whispers can come at any time: during a morning walk, in the middle of a busy workday, while driving, or even during a moment of quiet reflection before sleep. They are not interruptions. They are *invitations.*

But to truly experience their fullness, it is essential to cultivate *consistent space for God*—a time of sacred solitude, free from distractions. Whether it's ten minutes in the morning or a quiet moment before bed, there is no perfect formula. What matters is your *intention to be with Him.*

Jesus modeled this beautifully. He often withdrew to mountains and quiet places to pray, choosing solitude as the setting for connection with the Father. One of Jesus' extraordinary moments to retreat from external relationships and situations was at Gethsemane where he prayed fervently and alone while grappling with His life's purpose and destiny.

Following His example, find your own sacred space. It may be a prayer chair, a garden path, a quiet room, or simply a window where sunlight comes in. Wherever it is, return to it often, for there God will be waiting.

In that stillness, Psalm 23:1-4 becomes more than a poetic promise, it becomes your lived experience:

> *"The Lord is my shepherd, I lack nothing. He makes me lie down in green pastures; He leads me beside quiet waters. He refreshes my soul. He guides me along the right paths for His name's sake. Even though I walk through the darkest valley, I will fear no evil, for You are with me."*

This is the blessing of your sacred space:

> Green pastures in your mind.
> Quiet waters in your soul.
> Renewal through whispers.
> Guidance through presence.
> And courage through love.

> Let your life be led by the gentle rhythm of *Divine Whispers*.
> Let your soul be still.
> God is speaking.
> **Listen well.**

FINAL PRAYER OF BLESSING

WHISPER TO MY SOUL

Gracious and Ever-Present God,
Thank You for dwelling within the sacred space of my soul.
Thank You for the whispers that guide me, comfort me, correct me, and call me deeper into relationship with You.
In moments of silence, help me to hear You.
In moments of chaos, remind me You are near.
When I am weary, be the still waters that restore my soul.
When I am uncertain, whisper truth into the depths of my being.
Teach me to live aware of Your presence,
to be fully present with You,
to wait with quiet anticipation,
and to receive revelation that only comes through love.
Let my soul remain a holy temple, uncluttered and open—
a sanctuary where Your voice is welcome and Your

Spirit reigns.
May each day bring new opportunities to know You, trust You, and follow the sound of Your sacred voice.
I surrender my worries, my questions, and my striving.
Whisper peace.
Whisper strength.
Whisper purpose.
Whisper love.
Amen.

APPENDIX

A. Divine Whispers Life Journal

Throughout your life, God's voice has been present, sometimes as a gentle nudge and other times as a clear call. The goal of this journal is to help you *recognize, remember, and record* the moments when you sensed God speaking to your inner soul.

This isn't about dramatic encounters only, it's about noticing the subtle ways God has guided you through peace, clarity, redirection, and love. By looking back, you can better see the threads of His faithfulness and how they weave into your life's purpose.

Step 1: Map Your Life Timeline with Divine Whispers

Think of your life in stages. For each stage below, write down the moments when you believe God was whispering to you. Use the **Divine Whisper Categories** as a guide or create your own based on your experiences.

Divine Whisper Categories

- **Whispers of comfort** – times you felt God's peace in seasons of fear, loss, or hardship.

- **Whispers of calling** – moments you sensed God's direction for your gifts, mission, or next steps.
- **Whispers of clarity** – times God brought understanding or truth in a confusing situation.
- **Whispers of correction** – loving re-directions from God that kept you aligned with His ways.
- **Whispers of love** – encounters where you felt God's deep affection—whether directly in prayer or through others.

Life Stage	Divine Whispers You Remember
Childhood	
Adolescence	
Young Adulthood	
Present Day	

Step 2: Reflect on Each Whisper

Once you've written your whispers for each stage, take time to reflect on what they meant. Let these questions guide your journaling: What was happening in your life at the time? (Describe the events, emotions, or decisions you were facing.) What do you believe God was whispering to you? (Think about the message, comfort, guidance, or truth you sensed.) How did that experience shape your relationship with God? (Did it deepen your trust? Reveal something new? Challenge you to grow?)

Final Encouragement

This journal is more than a record; it's a spiritual treasure map. As you write, you may start to see patterns of God's presence that you didn't recognize before. You may find reminders of His love in the moments you least expected it, or clarity about your purpose that was quietly forming all along. God's whisper has been with you since the very beginning. This is your opportunity to tune in more deeply and let those memories strengthen your walk with Him.

B. Chapter-Based Scripture Index

CHAPTER ONE:
BE STILL – GOD IS IN HIS HOLY TEMPLE

1. **Psalm 46:10** – *"Be still, and know that I am God; I will be exalted among the nations, I will be exalted in the earth."*
   - Reminds you to quiet your heart and acknowledge God's sovereignty.
2. **Exodus 14:14** – *"The Lord will fight for you; you need only to be still."*
   - A call to trust God's power over your circumstances.
3. **Psalm 37:7** – *"Be still before the Lord and wait patiently for him; do not fret when people succeed in their ways, when they carry out their wicked schemes."*
   - Encourages patient trust even when life feels unfair.
4. **Habakkuk 2:20** – *"The Lord is in his holy temple; let all the earth be silent before him."*
   - A sacred invitation to reverent stillness before God.

CHAPTER TWO:
YOUR SPIRITUAL UMBILICAL CORD

1. **John 15:5** – *"I am the vine; you are the branches. If you remain in me and*

I in you, you will bear much fruit; apart from me you can do nothing."

- Illustrates your dependence on Christ for life and purpose.

2. **Colossians 2:6-7** – *"So then, just as you received Christ Jesus as Lord, continue to live your lives in him, rooted and built up in him…"*

- Encourages deep spiritual rootedness in Christ.

3. **Isaiah 41:10** – *"So do not fear, for I am with you … I will strengthen you and help you."*

- This affirms God's sustaining presence.

4. **Jeremiah 17:7-8** – *"But blessed is the one who trusts in the Lord… they will be like a tree planted by the water …"*

- A picture of God's spiritual nourishment.

CHAPTER THREE: SACRED PLACE

1. **1 Corinthians 3:16–17** – *"Don't you know that you yourselves are God's temple and that God's Spirit dwells in your midst?"*

- Declares the sacredness of your inner life as God's dwelling place.

2. **Psalm 27:4** – *"One thing I ask from the Lord … that I may dwell in the house of the Lord all the days of my*

life…"
- Expresses a longing to remain in God's presence.
3. **Matthew 6:6** – *"But when you pray, go into your room, close the door and pray to your Father…"*
   - Encourages personal, intimate communion with God.
4. **Hebrews 10:22** – *"Let us draw near to God with a sincere heart and with the full assurance that faith brings…"*
   - Calls for confident closeness with God.

CHAPTER FOUR: AN AWAKENING

1. **Ephesians 5:14** – *"Wake up, sleeper, rise from the dead, and Christ will shine on you."*
   - A spiritual call to awaken to God's light.
2. **Romans 13:11** – *"… The hour has already come for you to wake up from your slumber, because our salvation is nearer now than when we first believed."*
   - Urges readiness and being alert to God's timing.
3. **Isaiah 60:1** – *"Arise, shine, for your light has come, and the glory of the Lord rises upon you."*
   - Encourages stepping into the

fullness of God's presence.

4. **Psalm 119:105** – *"Your word is a lamp to my feet and a light to my path."*
   - Reminds you of Scripture's guiding light in spiritual awakening.

CHAPTER FIVE: DIVINE WHISPERS

1. **1 Kings 19:12** – *"And after the earthquake a fire; but the Lord was not in the fire: and after the fire a still small voice."*
   - Highlights God's gentle way of speaking that often comes in quietness.

2. **Isaiah 30:21** – *"Whether you turn to the right or to the left, your ears will hear a voice behind you, saying, 'This is the way; walk in it.'"*
   - Shows God's whisper as personal guidance in life's decisions.

3. **John 14:26** – *"But the Advocate, the Holy Spirit, whom the Father will send in my name, will teach you all things and will remind you of everything I have said to you."*
   - Reveals the Holy Spirit's role in bringing God's whisper to remembrance and understanding.

4. **Job 33:14–15** – *"For God does speak—now one way, now another—though no one perceives it. In a*

dream, in a vision of the night, when deep sleep falls on people as they slumber in their beds."

- This emphasizes God's diverse and sometimes subtle ways of speaking.

5. **Psalm 85:8** – *"I will listen to what God the Lord says; he promises peace to his people, his faithful servants— but let them not turn to folly."*

- Encourages a posture of listening for God's whisper that brings peace.

CHAPTER SIX: ACTS TOWARD RELATIONSHIP

1. **Micah 6:8** – *"He has shown you... what does the Lord require of you? To act justly and to love mercy and to walk humbly with your God."*

- Summarizes God's call to live out relationship through action.

2. **John 15:12-13** – *"My command is this: Love each other as I have loved you..."*

- Highlights love as the core of God-centered relationships.

3. **James 2:17** – *"Faith by itself, if it is not accompanied by action, is dead."*

- This verse links faith to tangible expression.

4. **1 John 3:18** – *"Let us not love with*

words or speech but with actions and in truth."

- Calls for authentic, active love.

CHAPTER SEVEN: WHEN GOD'S WHISPER REVEALS UR-NIQUE PURPOSE

1. **Jeremiah 1:5** – *"Before I formed you in the womb I knew you, before you were born I set you apart…"*
   - Affirms God's intentional design and calling from the very beginning.

2. **Ephesians 2:10** – *"For we are God's handiwork, created in Christ Jesus to do good works, which God prepared in advance for us to do."*
   - Emphasizes God's preordained purpose for every believer.

3. **Proverbs 19:21** – *"Many are the plans in a person's heart, but it is the Lord's purpose that prevails."*
   - Reminds you that God's purpose is the guiding force of your life.

4. **Romans 8:28** – *"And we know that in all things God works for the good of those who love him, who have been called according to his purpose."*
   - Connects life events to God's overarching plan for our good.

5. **Isaiah 49:1** – *"… Before I was born the Lord called me; from my mother's womb he has spoken my name."*

- Declares God's intimate, personal call from the very start.

C. Topical Scripture Index

How to Use This Index

This Topical Scripture Index is designed to help you quickly find Bible verses that connect with key themes from *Divine Whispers Within*. Each topic gathers passages you can meditate on during prayer, journaling, or moments of quiet reflection.

Here are a few ways to use it:

1. **Focus your devotional time** – choose one topic that speaks to your current spiritual need and read through its verses slowly, allowing God's Word to speak into your heart.

2. **Scripture meditation** – select one verse and repeat it throughout the day, pausing to reflect on its meaning in different moments.

3. **Prayer alignment** – use the verses as starting points for your prayers, letting them guide your conversation with God.

4. **Personal study** – explore the surrounding chapter or passage for deeper context, noting what God might be highlighting for you.

Let this index be more than a reference tool—let it become a pathway to deepen your awareness of God's voice, presence, and purpose in your life.

Stillness and Presence

These verses remind us to quiet our minds,

rest in God's presence, and trust His timing. They encourage us to step away from the noise and distractions to be fully attentive to Him.

- Psalm 46:10
- Exodus 14:14
- Psalm 37:7
- Habakkuk 2:20

Sacred Space and Temple Imagery

These passages highlight the truth that our bodies and lives are sacred spaces where God's Spirit dwells. They draw on biblical imagery of the temple to emphasize holiness, intimacy, and reverence in our relationship with Him.

- 1 Corinthians 3:16–17
- 1 Corinthians 6:19–20
- Ephesians 2:21–22
- Genesis 2:7

Hearing God/Divine Whispers

These scriptures illustrate how God communicates with His people, sometimes in subtle, quiet ways, and invite us to listen with open hearts. They encourage sensitivity to His Spirit in everyday life.

- John 10:27
- Isaiah 30:21
- 1 Kings 19:12
- Jeremiah 33:3

Intimacy with God

These verses emphasize deep, personal

connection with God. They invite us to draw near, remain in His presence, and experience His Spirit bearing witness within us.

- John 15:4
- James 4:8
- Romans 8:16
- Psalm 139:7–10

Waiting and Anticipation

These passages speak to the spiritual discipline of waiting on God with trust and expectation, knowing that His timing is perfect and His voice will bring clarity.

- Psalm 130:5
- Psalm 37:7
- Habakkuk 2:20
- Isaiah 30:21

CONTACT INFORMATION

For consultation, presentations, and workshops

Email
vernonf@pitt.edu

Website
https://franklinconsultingandtrainings.com

Facebook
https://www.facebook.com/vernon.franklin.9/

LinkedIn
https://www.linkedin.com/in/vernon-franklin-ed-d-0b7644/

www.ingramcontent.com/pod-product-compliance
Lightning Source LLC
LaVergne TN
LVHW051509070426
835507LV00022B/3012